Old MUSSELBURGH

by
Donald Lindgren

The Musselburgh Races have been an important event in the sporting life of the community for almost two centuries, and their popularity is illustrated in this picture of Race Day, attended by a crowd of thousands.

MUSSELBURGH RACES.

ORDER BY THE MAGISTRATES.

27th & 28th September 1894.

All Coaches plying for hire and taking up Passengers for the Races shall draw up in Single Line, under the direction of the Police, as follows:—

1. The front of rank on the South Side of Princes Street at Waverley Market, with Horses' heads looking East.

2. The rear of rank to be from the North end of the Waverley Bridge, West side, extending Southwards to, and into, West Market Street, North side.

No Coach shall leave Waverley Bridge for Stance at Waverley Market till called by Police.

All canvassing, loitering, and taking up Passengers at unauthorised Stances will be dealt with in accordance with Bye-Laws for Regulation of Edinburgh Omnibus Traffic.

BY ORDER,

A. CAMPBELL,

26th September 1894. *Depute City Clerk.*

© Donald Lindgren 2001
First published in the United Kingdom, 2001,
by Stenlake Publishing
Telephone / Fax: 01290 551122

ISBN 1 84033 167 4

ACKNOWLEDGEMENTS

I wish to thank Oliver van Helden and Stenlake Publishing for their encouragement, support and suggestion in the first place that I write this book. I am also indebted to Alex Ritchie, David Finlayson, Myra Law, Jane and John Fairnie, and Peggy Livingstone for photographs and information. There are others as well, too numerous to mention by name, but I appreciate all those who helped me in any way. This is the fourth book I have written on Musselburgh and it is a place that is very dear to my heart, having been my home and 'parish' for over a third of a century. I hope that this book will bring some of the pleasure to the people of Musselburgh that people of the burgh have brought to me.

The publishers would like to thank Robert Grieves for providing the pictures that appear on pages 26 and 27.

Left: This poster relates to the races of 27 and 28 September 1894. It describes an order by the magistrates and Depute City Clerk of Edinburgh outlining the arrangements for travel to the racecourse from Princes Street and Waverley Market 'with Horses' heads looking East'. Although officially recognised as a racecourse in 1816, races have taken place on the same site in Musselburgh for hundreds of years on Fair Day. Today the course is one of the major Flat Racing and National Hunt venues in Great Britain having 22 races days throughout the year. In 1995 the new hospitality stand was opened by Her Majesty the Queen. More recently the Princess Royal opened The Tote. Interestingly, the ground on which the racecourse stands is owned by the people of Musselburgh, but the buildings belong to the East Lothian Racing Board. Racing at Musselburgh now takes place more frequently than ever, and it is not unusual for the people of the burgh to see their course on national television.

INTRODUCTION

When the people of Musselburgh sing the chorus of Alexander Innes's *Musselburgh Song*:

> Musselburgh was a burgh when Edinburgh was nane,
> And Musselburgh will be a burgh when Edinburgh's gane.

they really mean it because Musselburgh dates back to the time of the Romans, who occupied Inveresk Hill over 2,000 years ago. Evidence of a Bronze Age settlement has also been found in the area. When, as the Leader of the Musselburgh Ministers Fraternal, I was asked several years ago by East Lothian District to consecrate a new section of Inveresk Cemetery, a Roman site was being excavated by the National Museum only 50 feet from where I was conducting the service. There are other Roman remains in the burgh such as the Roman bridge, which at one time formed part of the main thoroughfare between Edinburgh and London. Chambers in his *History of the Rebellion of 1745–46* speaks of this historic bridge: 'there is a structure over which all of noble or kingly birth, that had approached Edinburgh for at least a thousands years, must certainly have passed over'. History also records that there has been a place of worship on Inveresk Hill since Roman times and the present church, St Michael's, dates from AD 519, when it was founded by St Modwenna. During the Reformation the great preacher, reformer and martyr George Wishart (1513–1546) preached at Inveresk and was protected by armed bodyguards, one of whom was his friend John Knox, Scotland's greatest reformer.

Musselburgh also has connections with royalty, and Mary Queen of Scots surrendered to the rebel lords on Carberry Hill in 1567. Our present Queen Elizabeth and her sister Princess Margaret, as children, visited their aunt and uncle, Lord and Lady Elphinstone, at Carberry Tower. The late Lady Elphinstone was the sister of Queen Elizabeth, the Queen Mother.

The town has a remarkable history in the realms of sport, manufacturing, agriculture and fishing, and in 1954 Sir Compton Mackenzie paid tribute to the burgh at the Sashing ceremony of the Honest Lad and Lass when he referred to the 'genius of Musselburgh'. There are so many historic events and firsts in Musselburgh's history that an entire volume could be written on that subject alone, and this short introduction cannot do them justice. However, I will recall a few.

Many call Musselburgh the home of golf, and the game has been played on the old Links, now surrounded by the racecourse, since 1672. At one time the town was home to four famous clubs, of which the Royal Musselburgh was founded in 1774 and moved to Prestongrange in 1925. Because of crowded conditions in the city, three distinguished Edinburgh clubs relocated to Musselburgh and built their clubhouses, which still stand today, on Balcarres Road. These were The Honourable Company of Edinburgh Golfers, which came to the town in 1836 and in 1891 moved to Muirfield at Gullane (taking the Open championship with them), Bruntsfield Links Golfing Society (arrived in Musselburgh in 1861 and left *c*.1900), and the Edinburgh Burgess Golfing Society (arrived in Musselburgh in 1873 and moved to their own course at Barnton in 1894). A Musselburgh man, Willie Park, became the first Open champion in 1860 when the contest was called the Open Championship of the World and went on to win it three more times. His son Willie Park Jr. brought distinction to the world of golf through his championship wins and was also a golf club maker of distinction, as well as a world-famous designer of golf courses responsible for projects throughout Britain, America and other parts of the world. Willie Park Jr. was the last Musselburgh man to win the Open. Also in the field of sport the Queen's bodyguards in Scotland, the Royal Company of Archers, compete to this very day on Musselburgh old Links for one of the most ancient sporting trophies in the world, The Silver Arrow. The date on the earliest medal on this magnificent trophy is 1603.

Brunton's Wire Mill produced the cables for many of the suspension bridges of the world including the Forth Road Bridge, Quebec's suspension bridge, the Humber suspension bridge and the Bosporus Bridge in Istanbul. Linking Europe with Asia, this is the fourth largest suspension bridge in the world and incorporates 28,000 feet of steel rope manufactured in Musselburgh.

In 1812 John Paterson, who had a small business in Musselburgh, having watched fishermen at the harbour making nets by hand invented and patented the 'Scottish Net Loom', a machine that for the first time allowed nets to be woven with single and double knots. This was the first automatic net loom in the world. When John Paterson died the business was taken over by J. & W. Stuart, who moved the factory to beside the River Esk to take advantage of its water power, and went on to develop a world famous business with operations in Stonehaven, Buckie, Fraserburgh, Lowestoft, Portugal, Angola and Australia. They made nets the size of football pitches as well as smaller salmon nets for the Pacific coast of North America. A herring purse seine net made by Stuarts weighed 11 tons, measured 620 yards by 170 yards and could hold 200 tons of fish. The company's products were marketed under 'Hercules' and 'Star' brands, and were known throughout the world for quality and workmanship.

David Lowe, market gardener, grew fruit and vegetables for the tables of Edinburgh and beyond but was most famous for the development of the Musselburgh leek. It is said that the Romans brought leeks to the town, but today it is David Lowe's that are famous and Musselburgh leek seeds can be bought all over the world.

Fisherrow harbour is situated on the site of the original Roman harbour. The men of Fisherrow have earned their living from the sea for generations, and also served their country during the Napoleonic and two world wars. In the eighteenth century they protected the east coast of Scotland and the Firth of Forth and were rewarded for their faithful service with a medal which is worn at the Fishermen's walk by the President of the Fishermen's Association.

Despite being a relatively small town, Musselburgh has made gigantic contributions to the worlds of sport, industry, fishing and invention. It is a bonnie town, it is a fascinating town and it is a town that not only has a long history, but a people who can be proud of their heritage and of the contribution they continue to make today.

Sir David Lowe was not only provost of Musselburgh but also a very well known market gardener who developed the famous Musselburgh leek. To my amazement I have been able to find Musselburgh leek seeds on sale in seed shops wherever I have travelled in the world. Not long ago I took my grand nephew, Eric, into a very posh gardening shop in the largest mall in the world, The Mall of America in Minneapolis, Minnesota and there we saw Musselburgh leek seeds for sale. Eric could not believe it. This is Sir David Lowe & Sons entry into the 1935 Riding of the Marches parade. It was Sir David's development of his famous leek that gave rise to the saying that Musselburgh is known for the 3 L's: 'Leeks, Loonies, and Liars'. Of course we know that this is not true, but it does make a good story. There were, however, five lunatic asylums in the burgh!

This photograph, taken in 1912 outside No. 11 Eskside West, shows the cart and horse owned by David Finlayson (known as Coal Davie) ready to enter the procession for the Riding of the Marches festival. The horse is decked out in its finest harness and decorations for this special event, while its owner stands alongside proudly. David's three-year-old son (also called David but known as Daw) sits waiting for the moment when they will begin the procession, holding the reigns in anticipation of a happy day. His father, who started his business in Fisherrow around the turn of last century, and his ancestors thereafter, have been prominent and successful Fisherrow businessmen for a hundred years. David's grandson, also named David, kindly provided me with this and other photographs for inclusion in this book. It is his father who sits on the lorry, and at the age of three did not know that one day he would have a son named after him.

David Finlayson's band was famous throughout East Lothian and played at wedding receptions, Masonic dances, miners' socials, and British Legion events. In this photograph, taken by the River Esk, they are playing for the Sashing of the Honest Lad and Lass, held at the beginning of Festival Week in July. Members of the band are, from left to right: Jock Finlayson, brother of David, on drums, unknown trumpeter, David Finlayson, Joe McMillan and Tommy McEwan, all playing the accordion. Those seated in the front row are the Honest Toun's Association party.

On the day of the Coronation of Queen Elizabeth in 1953 street parties were held in neighbourhoods throughout the United Kingdom and the Commonwealth. One such party took place in Musselburgh at the foot of Kilwinning Place and Dambrae, and this picture features some of the mothers and children of the neighbourhood. Also in the picture are a doll, a cat and a puppy! Those featured include Ann Brooks, Jeanette Smith, the Bourhill twins, Jock Owenson, Jimmy Pride, Catherine Porter, Isobel Edwards, Josephine Ferguson, Elizabeth Robinson, Heather Cummings, Catherine Eadie, her son Alister Eadie, Helen Pryde, Helen Murray, Kate Murray, Marina Buckerly, Betty Ferguson, Ann Ross, Maureen Porter and Maureen Murray.

This bridge over the River Esk must surely be the oldest structure in Musselburgh, dating as it does from Roman times. In 1809 the bridge needed to be repaired and when the face of one of the buttresses was removed for inspection Roman construction was revealed, putting its ancient origins beyond any doubt. Today it is only a footbridge, but in past centuries it formed part of the main road from Edinburgh to London. While the Scottish army was passing over this bridge after their disastrous defeat at the Battle of Pinkie in Musselburgh in 1547 Lord Graham, eldest son of the Earl of Montrose, and several others were killed upon it by a shot from the English vessels lying off the mouth of the Esk in the Firth of Forth. Bonnie Prince Charlie, together with his Highland army, marched over the bridge on his way to victory at the Battle of Prestonpans in 1745. The much-loved landmark is floodlit on special occasions.

This picture was taken from the tower of St Peter's Scottish Episcopal Church and shows the part of the High Street that opens out into a wide avenue. In the left foreground cabs for hire can be seen lined up waiting for customers. The old town hall with its Dutch-like tower is in the distance; for many years the tower housed a clock given to the burgh in 1496 by Dutch traders in appreciation of the commerce between the two communities. Next to the town hall is the tolbooth, built in the late sixteenth century with stone taken from Loretto Chapel, remnants of which still stand in the grounds of Loretto School (and after which the school is named). This chapel was one of the earliest religious houses in Scotland, and when stones from it were used to build the tolbooth, a secular building, in 1590, the town burgesses were annually excommunicated by the Pope for two centuries afterwards as a punishment.

Who ever heard of Wonder Street in Musselburgh? Probably very few people, because this rare postcard dates from the start of the twentieth century, and since then Wonder Street has become Inveresk Road and all but two of the buildings in the picture have been demolished. Today you will still see children in this area, but instead of playing in the street they are more likely to be going to the Grammar School, which was build on the left-hand side many years after this postcard was produced. At one time the premises of Adam Clark, shoemaker, James Cathie, tailor, and Robert Clark, cattle merchant were all in Wonder Street. None of these have survived, although Our Lady of Loretto Chapel, visible in the distance, is still very much in existence.

Wonder Street, Newbiggin, Musselburgh.

THE PILLARS MUSSELBURGH

This photograph was taken in 1905 and gives an excellent view of the east entrance to the town known as Pinkie Pillars. St Peter's Scottish Episcopal Church is on the right. In the left foreground is one of the oldest buildings in the burgh. At one time it was known as the Commercial Inn and had stables behind it – in the early twentieth century it advertised carriages, gigs, and dog carts for hire. The house next to it was reputed to have once been the residence of the French Ambassador.

The Mercat Cross was erected on the site of an old well and is surmounted by a lion rampant holding the arms of the burgh. It marks the spot where the 'Midraw' stood, a row of houses that once ran down the middle of High Street. At this same site in times past, debates, markets, and political meetings took place. A particularly fascinating event unfolded here and in the oldest hostelry in the burgh, the Musselburgh Arms Hotel. This is recorded, in part, in the minutes of the burgh records of 1831. The story goes that six resurrectionists (more commonly called body-snatchers) came from Edinburgh to steal bodies from Inveresk Cemetery to sell to Dr Knox of the Royal Infirmary for his anatomy classes. They went to the Musselburgh Arms for a drink and to hire a gig to transport these bodies. Unfortunately they got drunk and revealed their plans to others at the inn. While they were at the cemetery, the local militia were informed and went there immediately, catching the culprits loading bodies into the gig. In their zeal they brought the empty gig back to the Mercat Cross and set it on fire, not knowing that it belonged to Mr Campbell, proprietor of the Musselburgh Arms. Angry at the destruction of his property he asked the town council, on 14 July 1831, to pay for the gig to be replaced. They paid up and an order from the Commercial Bank for £22 10s. was made out in favour of Mr Campbell.

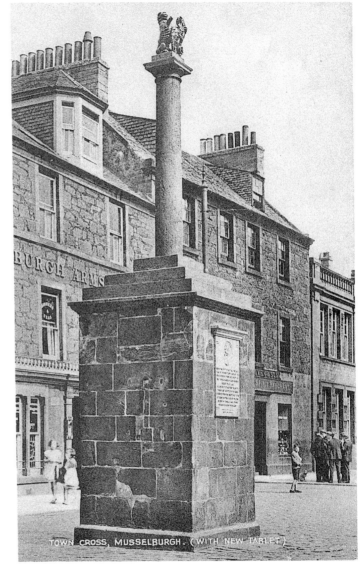

TOWN CROSS, MUSSELBURGH. (WITH NEW TABLET.)

The Mall, Musselburgh

On the west side of the Mall, by the stone bridge, stands a memorial raised by public subscription to one of the great and much-loved citizens of the burgh, Dr David Macbeth Moir (1798–1851), who for a lifetime served its inhabitants as doctor and friend. Even Charles Dickens sent some money towards this tribute to his friend. During a long cholera epidemic in the town in 1830 the doctor worked day and night, and was so devoted to the citizens of the burgh that for 13 years he never left its boundaries. Dr Moir was also a well-known author of his day who wrote several best-selling novels, as well as contributing to *Blackwood's Magazine* under the name of Delta. The memorial, comprising a 20-foot pedestal bearing an 8-foot statue of the doctor, was dedicated in December of 1853. It was the work of a distinguished sculptor of the day, Alexander Handyside Ritchie, who had his studio in the village of Inveresk. Ritchie studied under the greatest sculptor of Denmark, Bertle Thorwaldson, and became a favourite pupil. The pedestal carries a suitable inscription in tribute to a wonderful friend and doctor to the people of Musselburgh.

This magnificent drinking fountain, which is just over 100 years old, was given to the burgh by David T. Wright, merchant of Riddle's Close, Leith, but a native of Musselburgh. When it was presented to the town Mr Wright said that it was as a memento to 'auld lang syne'. The fountain, which is situated by the Hollies Day Centre at the east end of the bridge over the Esk, was designed by James Simpson, architect, and executed by his son, George Simpson of Leith (also an architect). The octagonal design incorporates four drinking basins and shields bearing the coats of arms of Musselburgh, St Michael (the patron saint of the burgh), Randolph Earl of Moray, who died in the burgh in July 1332, and David Wright. Until recently Musselburgh's only war memorial was at St Michael's Church, and this included only the names of the fallen from Inveresk parish. A proposal was put forward recently for a memorial that listed the names of all those from the burgh who had lost their lives in the two world wars. On Remembrance Sunday 1999, this fountain became the official war memorial for the burgh when four beautiful bronze tablets, bearing the names of all those who had given their lives in battle, were dedicated with an appropriate service. No doubt Mr Wright would have approved.

At one time there were five picture houses in Musselburgh. The Central Cinema, located on the Mall just beside the High Kirk, was considered the best in town, and Logan's Picture House on New Street in Fisherrow, known locally as 'The Gaff', was considered by many to be the worst. Logan's Picture House was destroyed by fire in 1921. The Regal on Dalrymple Loan was the largest and the last to close, while the Hayweights in Fisherrow, run very well indeed by the Di Rollo family, still stands today as a bingo hall. The Pavilion Picture House was near the old town hall. It survived the hard times of the Depression when many were out of work, and on special occasions allowed customers admission to the cinema by handing in a jam jar. Some dispute this, but I have spoken personally to those who did indeed get into the Pavilion in this way. This picture shows the Pavilion after it had undergone a name-change to the Arcadia (although the photograph shows that the bar next door is still named the Pavilion). Also seen is tram No. 32 on its way to the post office on Princes Street, Edinburgh.

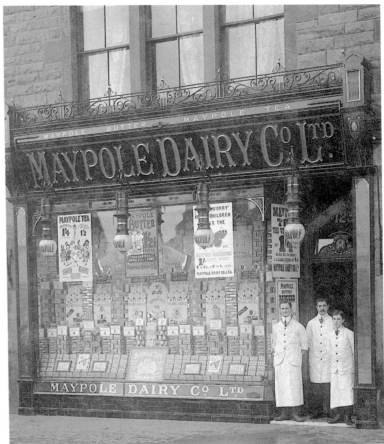

An SMT bus, a tram, and a van cause a temporary blockage on the High Street. Today the street is a nightmare to navigate because of the volume of traffic that passes through the town. Tram No. 411 is heading eastwards towards Port Seton, which was the terminus from 1909 to 1928 (from 1928 onwards trams terminated at Levenhall). Trams ceased to run in the early 1950s having found themselves unable to compete with private bus operators such as SMT.

The Maypole Dairy was on North High Street where the co-op chemist's stands today. It sold butter, cheese and tea, and its staff provided a personal service that was much appreciated by customers, who came in for their necessities but also had a chat about the weather, the family and even sometimes their worries and problems. When you bought your pound of butter it was cut, patted into a square and wrapped. These days have now passed and people miss their local dairy, grocer, and hardware shop, and all those other wonderful places that provided a personal service.

This shop on Eskside West and Hercus Loan was a wonderland of sweets for the children who lived in the area, and its doors were seldom shut summer or winter. The proprietor sold sweets such as sour plums, squirrel gums, pan drops, 'ogy pogie eyes', and coloured sugar mice. The shop also supplied many things for the family including loose biscuits (you could buy as few or as many as you wanted), Robin Starch, Lyon's Tea, Coleman's Mustard, Rickets' Blue Dye and cigarettes of all kinds. It was lit by gaslight, but everyone was used to the flickering light because most homes were also lit by gas. When the photograph was taken in 1930 this shop was a hub of activity for the local community, and if you couldn't afford a sweet or two the proprietor wouldn't let you leave empty-handed. This shop and the one next door was owned by Archie McKinlay.

It has been a long time since trams have been seen on the streets of Musselburgh. The Hayweights (background) stood as a much-loved landmark in Fisherrow for many years. Peter Livingstone operated the Hayweights for over twenty years, weighing grain, hay and gravel and collecting revenue due to the town from this. Sadly the once-famous landmark has now been reduced to a 'roof on stilts' down by the River Esk and even the original clock, a gift from A. Black in 1908, has been removed.

This photograph was taken at Newhailes House on 3 July 1897. Newhailes was built by Sir David Dalrymple, an eminent Scottish lawyer, antiquarian and historian, who amassed what is considered to be the finest legal library in Scotland. Sir David took the title Lord Hailes of Newhailes when he was elevated to the House of Lords. Always public-spirited, the Dalrymple family contributed much to eighteenth and nineteenth century life through their good works. Newhailes House was recently acquired by The National Trust for Scotland and through their dedicated programme of restoration this magnificent building, one of the finest stately homes in the Lothians, will soon be open to the public. It is hoped that the famous library amassed by Lord Hailes (and now housed in the National Library in Edinburgh) will eventually be returned to Newhailes.

Loretto School is very much a part of Musselburgh and has been for over 180 years. It was founded as a school for boys by Revd Thomas Langholm in 1820, and throughout its long history many of these boys have served with distinction in the professions, in politics, and in the military. It was, however, when Dr Hely Almond became the owner of Loretto in 1862 that the foundations were laid for it to become one of the top public schools in Scotland. Dr Almond stressed the importance of independent thinking and physical fitness, and to this day these same principles are applied. The school's musical programme is second to none and the people of the burgh always enjoy the annual Christmas concert to which they are invited every year. This picture shows the Loretto Drum and Pipe Band of the Officers Training Corps.

Cadets and staff of 297 Squadron (Musselburgh) Air Training Corps photographed at their old headquarters at Goose Green. The squadron still meets today each Wednesday and Friday but in a newer building. The ATC was formed from the civilian organisation know as the Air League of the British Empire on 1 February 1941, and its members were given preference amongst those selected to join the Royal Air Force. Even today about 30 per cent of RAF recruits come from the ATC. 297 Squadron (Musselburgh) was one of the early squadrons and was formed in April of 1941. The first headquarters were in Musselburgh's municipal buildings, but parades were held later on Tuesday and Thursday evenings at the Grammar School. A. J. Corrie was the first squadron commander and the medical officer was Dr J. A. Aitchison. In its early days some of the young people met on Friday evenings, as well as the usual parade nights, for band practice when they brought along their harmonicas.

6TH MIDLOTHIAN
CUB PACK
1961 - 1962

This photograph of the 6th Midlothian Cub Pack was taken in 1962 in the hall of the Congregational Church, where the pack met under the leadership of Robert Langlands. He is standing in the back row with Alice Gordon to his right and Chrissie Smith on his left. Annie Muir, at the left of the third row, and Margaret Tait, at its right-hand end, were also leaders. It's hard to believe that many of the boys seen in this picture are grandfathers now. At the time young people attended the burgh's youth organisations in large numbers. Sadly, there are no longer any cub packs or scout troops in Musselburgh, and many believe this has had a detrimental affect on the burgh.

Musselburgh stands on a huge coalfield and it has been estimated that over the centuries there have been more than 150 coal workings around the burgh. One of the legacies of coal extraction has been subsidence, which still causes problems today because there are so many mine workings under the town. My own manse had to be built on a concrete platform for that reason. This photograph and the ones opposite are believed to show Smeaton colliery, which was taken over by Edinburgh Collieries in 1900. It is very sobering to note that it wasn't until 1842 that children under ten were outlawed from working in mines, and it is distressing to learn the kind of work they had to do. This included pulling carts through narrow passageways often only 24 to 30 inches high, and carrying loads of coal to the surface. Shifts often lasted twelve hours.

These photographs were taken around the turn of the century and show the extent of operations at Smeaton. All of the coal workings around Musselburgh have now ceased production. The major development of Monktonhall colliery was the last new pit to be opened (on 26 January 1965) and was expected to produce a million tons of coal a year, the bulk of it destined for Cockenzie power station. The power station still operates but today Monktonhall is closed. Cheaper foreign coal and nuclear power are among the factors that led to the decline of the once-famous coalfields of the Lothians. Many people whose sole means of making a living was coal mining were made redundant as the pits closed. Like fishing, mining was an occupation that ran in families for generations.

This picture shows the terminus at Joppa of the tramway systems operated by Musselburgh & District Electric Light and Traction Company Ltd. and the Edinburgh & District Tramway Company. The latter operated cable tramcars propelled using a system of underground cables, as the famous trams in San Francisco are to this day. The Musselburgh company ran electric trams using overhead wires. Travellers had to change at Joppa because the two systems were incompatible. By 1923 Edinburgh Corporation had converted the cable network to electricity, allowing through journeys. At one stage the Musselburgh company's electric trams ran as far east as Port Seton, but the section from there to Levenhall was abandoned in 1928. In 1931 Edinburgh Corporation took over the stretch from Joppa to Levenhall.

It's difficult to believe that this view shows Levenhall, where today there is a roundabout and the traffic is so busy that one takes one's life into one's hands when trying to cross the road. The fields on the left are now completely covered with houses. Mrs Forman's pub, on the right, is still popular with golfers playing on the ancient golf course on the adjacent links. It is also well-frequented by people from Levenhall and the Wimpey's (the name used by the people of the burgh for the estate built by builders Wimpey and Crudens) and Pinkie housing estate, who claim it as their local. Pinkie estate is so-named because its houses are built on the ground on which the famous Battle of Pinkie took place in 1547, when the Scots were defeated by the English invading armies. The open-top tram is heading west towards Musselburgh. The new motorised bus, with open upper deck crowded with people, has paused en route to Tranent for a photograph with the driver and conductor alongside.

This happy group were photographed in a charabanc belonging to James Bowen of the Mall, Musselburgh and South St Andrew Street Edinburgh, who operated a selection of day and half-day tours from Edinburgh. The 18-seater Albion Viking charabanc, SY 2692, was registered in 1924, and the driver on this occasion was Andrew McLeish. The tours continued until 1935 when the Scottish Motor Traction Company (SMT) took over Bowen's operations along with their depot in Musselburgh at the Mall. A newer building, which is now the depot for First Bus, stands on the same site.

No 265.

The cover of the timetable leaflet issued by Bowen's Motor Services of Musselburgh. This was one of the company's routes from Edinburgh to some of the mining villages around Musselburgh in the mid-1920s. Another ran from Chambers Street, Edinburgh to Elphinstone via Newcraighall, Musselburgh and Smeaton.

When the Musselburgh & District Electric Light and Traction Company Ltd. ceased to operate trams from Levenhall to Port Seton in 1928 it introduced a bus service between Edinburgh, Portobello, Musselburgh, Prestonpans and Port Seton, named 'Coast Line'. This Leyland Lion was typical of buses in their fleet and was one of several purchased in 1928 to replace the trams. In January 1937 Coast Line sold their service to the expanding Scottish Motor Traction Company (SMT) of Edinburgh.

Mitchell Place in Fisherrow no longer exists and today new houses occupy this site. In the background the houses of West Holmes Gardens, built around the turn of the twentieth century, are visible. The picture shows David Finlayson's coal lorry, with David himself standing on the right of the lorry holding a pipe. The man to his right is Peter Miller, who worked for the Finlaysons for many years. Leaning on the lorry in the left foreground is David's son Jock. David came to Fisherrow from Kelty in Fife as a young man at the beginning of the twentieth century. His family had dealt in glass there, but he decided to go into a new line of business and set up a very successful coal and scrap metal company, which thrives today in another form run by his great-grandson, also David Finlayson.

David Finlayson, known as Coal Davie to distinguish him from all the other Davids in the family, had just purchased this yard in New Street when this photo was taken. He is standing on the left with (from left to right) Beannie Brand, Nell Brown and her husband Bob Brown, and Betty Finlayson (David's daughter). Betty's brother Jock is in the cab of the lorry.

The small, tidal harbour of Fisherrow is impractical for large, modern fishing boats that travel long distances to the fishing grounds of the North Sea. During most of its history, however, Fisherrow was a working harbour, used both by fishing vessels and commercial sailing ships from the Baltic states, Norway, Prussia and Holland. This picture illustrates one of these ships, which often brought incoming cargoes of timber. They did not return empty, taking back as cargo and ballast salt from the salt pans of Joppa and Prestonpans, bricks and tiles from the brickworks of Prestongrange and Newcraighall, and locally-mined coal. There has been a harbour at Musselburgh since Roman times. For a time the harbour was situated at the mouth of the River Esk, but this location was found to be unsuitable and the harbour was relocated to its original site, where it is now used by pleasure boats.

This picture of the Fisherrow fleet in the harbour dates from 1901 when the extension to the harbour wall had not been built. An extension was necessary because of the strong swell that came into the harbour, particularly during storms, often breaking moorings and causing extensive damage. This was before the age of sophisticated navigation equipment and these small boats never sailed far from the shore. Their main fishing grounds were around the coast of the Firth of Forth, apart from during the annual herring season when they sailed much further afield. LH 903 was owned by W. Falconer and was called *Young Johns*. Today the few trawlers of the Fisherrow fleet are large vessels with expensive navigation equipment – as fish become scarcer the boats need to sail further to the fishing grounds and spend longer away at sea.

As everyone who sails on or lives near the Firth of Forth knows, it can be as gentle as a lamb, but in storm it can roar like a lion. In winter time at the harbour the waves can truly reach for the sky, and the whole seawall is frequently covered with walls of water. This picture was taken just off of Linkfield Road by the racecourse and ancient golf course after one such storm. The vessel that is stranded on dry land is believed to be Dunbar's lifeboat, which broke its moorings and was driven out into the firth by the ferocious storm. It was eventually beached high up on dry land at Musselburgh, and was later returned to service, although it was a huge task getting it back into the sea. One might well wonder if the writer of *Will your Anchor Hold* was thinking about such an incident when he wrote his much-loved hymn, which has a special place in the hearts of the fishing communities of Scotland.

Fisherrow harbour at low tide. Fishermen have never had an easy life, working in dangerous and unpleasant conditions to earn their living, but those of Fisherrow come from families that have worked at sea for generations and love their life. Diminished fish stocks and the introduction of fishing quotas have sadly contributed to the squeezing of many small family fishing businesses out of existence.

The people of Fisherrow have always been community-spirited and generous, and demonstrated these qualities by entering the annual Edinburgh Royal Infirmary Pageant held to collect funds for the hospital. This photograph was taken in 1936 when the Fisherrow entry won second prize in the pageant (although no doubt the participants gave a first-class donation of their time and talent). On this occasion the lorry was provided by Fisherrow scrap metal merchant David Finlayson, who is standing with his arm on his lorry. Amongst those on the lorry are: Peggy Thorburn, Betty Finlayson, Marion Langlands, Mary Langlands, George Wilson (beside his father Joe Wilson), Isa Douglas, Libby Langlands and Betty Wilson.

Fisherrow fishwives were noted for their hard work, honesty and devotion to their families. While their husbands were away at sea for most of the week they ran their own fish businesses, cared for their children, and handled the family money. Margaret Thorburn Fairnie, affectionately known as Maggie, was no exception. In addition to looking after her children and all the other weekly duties of a housewife she also travelled to Corstorphine, her area for selling fish in Edinburgh. In this picture she is filleting fish for the mother of a family who holds a plate out ready for it, while her children look on in fascination from the doorway. Maggie was a much-loved member of the fishing community, the eldest of eight children from one of Fisherrow's prominent families whose seafaring traditions go back for generations. She knew all about the hard work of getting up early, travelling by tram to the Newhaven fish market, and then going on to her customers in Corstorphine with almost a hundredweight of fish on her back.

Right: This photograph, which was taken in 1929, shows the skipper of *Albatross*, a trawler that came from Gardenstown in the north of Scotland to Fisherrow. Standing next to the skipper, on the right, is Johnny Ritchie, a member of another of Fisherrow's prominent fishing families. All of Johnny's brothers were fishermen, as were both of his sons. It was traditional to marry within the fishing community, and consequently cousins often married cousins, and families were so intermarried that the people of Fisherrow were related to just about every other member of the community.

Alex and Nancy Ritchie dressed up in their finest fishing clothes ready for the annual Fishermen's Walk, which was traditionally held on the first Friday in September each year. Alex wears his hand-knitted Guernsey jumper and Nancy is wearing traditional fishwives' costume. Today the Fisherrow fleet has all but disappeared, and like so many traditions that were once kept religiously, this festival has sadly ceased to take place. Alex served as President of the Fishermen's Association from 1986 until 1988, at which time the fishing community was still strong. It was traditional for the president to wear this medal, which was given to the community by the Crown and bears the following inscription: 'Presented to the Fishermen of Fisherrow in 1796 for their services against possible invasion from the enemy during the Napoleonic War'. Local fishermen patrolled the sea and coast from St Abb's Head in Berwickshire to Red Head in Angus.

It's the big day of the year for the fishing community of Fisherrow and the parade for the annual Fishermen's Walk has just begun after a service in the Seamen's Mission. Leading the parade from left to right are: missionary Hector Ronald, Muriel Fairnie, Sandy Ritchie (President of the Fishermen's Association), Katrine Liston and David Fairnie. For many years Hector Ronald was Fisherrow's chaplain, friend, and the driving force behind the mission on New Street. He was a spiritual leader of great sincerity and devotion, and the fishing community owe much to him. When Hector passed on, the Seamen's Mission, which he had served for over 30 years, lost its greatest supporter. Sadly the mission is no longer open.

The Fishermen's Walk was a celebration connected with the end of the summer fishing and associated with the traditional 'box meetings' common to many fishing communities in Scotland. The box, an example of which was formerly kept on display in the mission on New Street, held contributions made by the fishermen to be given to the poor, older people, the ill and those who were generally having a difficult time. This box could only be opened with three keys and these were held by three elected leaders of the fishing community. It was the tradition of the walk that on the way out from the mission on New Street (where a short service of thanksgiving was held by the missionary), the men, including the three key holders, walked at the front of the procession. On the way back men, women, and children were all mixed up together and many of the young fishermen, in particular, wore the shawl of a favourite girl! It was not unknown for this to be the beginning of a lifelong romance. The walk ended back at the mission with everyone singing the twenty-third psalm. In the evening a dance was held when those attending were required to wear traditional fisher dress. This 1984 photograph shows the band of the Black Watch leading the walk from the mission to the park in Loretto School grounds, which the folk of Fisherrow had been given the privilege of using years before when Pinkie House and grounds were owned by Sir Archibald Hope. When the house and lands were acquired from the Hope family by Loretto School it was with the understanding that the fishing community would always be allowed to use the park for their annual Fishermen's Walk.

Jane Fairnie, a hard-working member of the fishing community into which she married, learns something about the pipes from one of the pipe band members outside the mission in New Street before a Fishermen's Walk. She wears the fishwives costume that was handed down to her from her mother-in-law Phemia Fairnie. Sadly, with the dwindling of the fishing fleet and the high cost of holding the Fishermen's Walk it has not been held in recent years. It is hoped by many of the citizens of Musselburgh, particularly members of the fishing community, that it will be revived.

This photograph shows the fishermen of Fisherrow a long way from home, at Peel harbour on the Isle of Man. They were not strangers there and many made lifelong friends among the locals. Holidays were spent together both on the Isle of Man and in Fisherrow, and sometimes a marriage took place between the two communities. Every summer for many years during the herring fishing season, the Fisherrow fleet either travelled along the Forth and Clyde Canal (or through the magnificent Caledonian Canal further north) to reach the west coast and the Irish Sea. While sailing through the Caledonian Canal I was told by one of the lock keepers that he could always tell, from a distance, the boats from Fisherrow. This was not only because of their distinctive blue colour, but because they were the best-kept boats he saw on the canal.

All work and no play makes Jack a dull boy, or so the saying goes, and the young fishermen in this photograph knew what hard work was all about. However, when they were in harbour and all the work on board was finished there was time for some play. This photograph was taken on the Isle of Man at Glen Maye Cove near Peel, when the Fisherrow trawler fleet made their annual summer visit to the fishing grounds in the west and played football against the fishermen of Peel. It features from left to right, back row: Willie Wood, George Thorburn, Robert Brown, unknown, Jimmy Brown and Alex Brown. Front row: unknown, Tommy Ritchie with the ball, Andrew Ritchie and Dave Sherborn. Judging by the smiles on their faces it looks like they won, but even if they didn't it must have been a grand change from the hard work when they were on board at sea.

Right: The fishing boat *Supreme*, which belonged to the Watson family, held the distinction of being one of the first boats in Fisherrow harbour to have a wheelhouse and engine. Before that time sail was the usual means of power, and sailing vessels in the Fisherrow fleet can be seen in the background of this picture. On board *Supreme* from left to right are George Watson, William Watson, John Watson and Geordie Watson. Next to Geordie is his father Watty Watson, while the lad on the right is George Miller. Fishing was usually a family business with fathers, sons, uncles and cousins working together on the same boat. The two young lads in this photo would probably have joined a crew when they were older. It was the tradition on fishing boats that the youngest member of the crew became the cook until he was replaced by a new crew member.

The trawler *Fragrant* was built in 1948 for Robert Fairnie BEM, MBE and was the last boat to be built by Walter Reekie at his shipyard in St Monans in the East Neuk of Fife. The inset picture of *Fragrant*'s launch ceremony (in St Monans) shows Phemia Fairnie, wife of owner Robert, about to break the traditional bottle of champagne on the bow of the new boat. Standing beside her is Willie Gibson, a friend of the family. The lad by the name of Dow standing next to Willie wanted to be part of the launching ceremony.

After her launch *Fragrant* fished the Firth of Forth and Scottish coastal waters as far north as Inverness, from where she sailed through the Caledonian Canal to reach the west coast, sailing to the Isle of Man, Firth of Clyde and Outer Hebrides. From Fisherrow she also sailed southwards as far as Scarborough and Whitby. After Robert retired, his son John took over the fishing business. He is seen here, on the day *Fragrant* ended her career as a trawler in 1986 and was decommissioned. This picture and the ones opposite record the beginning and end of a Fisherrow trawler. The untold middle part of the story extended over 38 years and involved many tales of life on the waters around the coast of Britain.

The Fisherrow trawler *Brighter Dawn* (LH 219) is on a special mission. The year is 1947 and the crowd lining the harbour walls have come to watch the Harbour Ceremony, one of the many traditions of the Honest Toun Festival Week in July. The Honest Lad and Lass, who are elected by the people of Musselburgh and Fisherrow, are brought into the harbour from the Firth of Forth, with their attendants and Border friends, there to be welcomed by dignitaries and townspeople. It is also the tradition that they are served a plate of mussels, gathered just offshore at low tide.

The Fisherrow Choir was famous throughout Scotland and gave concerts at churches and organisations, where they were always warmly received. This photograph shows the choir singing at Fisherrow harbour with Mrs Brodie conducting and Nancy Scott at the piano. A huge crowd has gathered to hear them sing and enjoy the ceremony for the Honest Lad and Lass. The women's traditional fisher costumes never failed to delight their audiences. Mrs Brodie conducted the choir, which sadly no longer exists, for many years. As time goes by many age-old traditions are being lost and this can only be regretted.

When Sandy Livingstone of Fisherrow was nine years old he told his father that one day he was going to sail around the world. His father said to him, 'Sandy, that's a pipe dream'. Unfortunately Mr Livingstone was not alive when, as seen in this photograph, his son sailed into Fisherrow harbour on 15 September 1989 after a 20,000 mile voyage in *Odyssey*, the boat he had built with his own hands at his home in Whangarei, North Island, New Zealand. His wife Joan and two daughters, Morag (9) and Suzanne (13) had made the journey with him. They sailed across the Tasman Sea to Brisbane, along the Great Barrier Reef, across the Indian Ocean to Durban and Cape Town, then continued via the South Atlantic, Cape Verde Islands and North Atlantic to the English Channel, North Sea and Firth of Forth. After clearing customs at Granton *Odyssey* came into Fisherrow, the village where Sandy had been born. Sandy and his family stayed for two and a half years and then returned by way of Madeira, the Caribbean, the Panama Canal, the Pacific Ocean (stopping off at Tonga), arriving back at their home port in New Zealand in November of 1992 after a voyage of 17,000 miles.

The River Esk, which runs through the burgh dividing it into the two communities of Musselburgh and Fisherrow, empties into the Firth of Forth. It seldom freezes and the scene shown here is rare indeed. The photograph was taken in 1897 when the river froze hard enough to use as a curling rink, and a game was arranged between the Musselburgh and Dalkeith clubs. Musselburgh Curling Club, founded in 1816, is the third oldest curling club in the world and still meets today at rinks in Edinburgh. At least one player in this early photograph is using the modern type of broom, although the rest are using traditional corn brooms, which were standard a hundred years ago.

In 1901 the Musselburgh Congregational Church celebrated the centenary of the building of its church on Link Street, and this photograph of its distinguished-looking deacons was taken during those celebrations. This was a time when churches played a very important part, not only in the spiritual life of the community, but also in its social life, and had full congregations at their many services on Sunday and during the week. The Congregational Church in Musselburgh was no exception and has always had a much greater influence on the people of the town than its size would suggest. Its Sunday school was often the best-attended in town and even today people from all churches speak about their association in their youth with the Congregational Church Sunday school. The deacons featured in this photograph are back row, from left to right: Robert Lambert and J. Arnott. Middle row: R. Burns, J. M. Gibb, treasurer, J. W. Muskett, secretary, D. Watson. Front row: F. Lamb, A. M'Leay, Revd David Farquharson, minister, J. Anderson, T. Dobson.

Almost 100 years after the previous centenary celebrations in 1901 the Congregational Church celebrated not the bicentenary of its building but of its formation as a church in 1798. To begin with its members had met in a barn at the top of Link Street not far from the present church building, which is now 200 years old. In 1998 there were all kinds of celebrations. Two church services were broadcast throughout Scotland on television, and a church dinner was held in the Brunton Hall when former members and invited guests from abroad joined the congregation in celebration. Various other events were held during the year to celebrate 200 years of service to Fisherrow, Musselburgh and through their support of their Missionary Society throughout the world. The deacons in this photograph are, left to right, back row: Raymond Denholm, Norrie Cleeton, Ann McKillop, Agnes Spence, secretary, Jim Brown, Andrew Reid. Front row: Jim Frame, Susan Johnstone, president, Revd Donald Lindgren BA BTh MTh, minister (and author of this book), Christine Cranston, Ian Johnstone, treasurer. Robert Langlands, George Fairley, Bill Mullen and David Caven were not able to be present. Photograph by Jack Crombie of Prestonpans.

Shortly after the Second World War a municipal bowling green was built on New Street, and since this photograph was taken in 1956 a commodious clubhouse has been built. In the background stand large houses in Mountjoy Terrace, situated close to the Firth of Forth. There are a number of bowling clubs and greens in Musselburgh, many of them associated with the town's various works. Indoor carpet bowling is held in the Brunton Hall each week during the winter.